Original title:
Umbral Wisps Beneath the Dragon Bolt

Copyright © 2025 Swan Charm
All rights reserved.

Author: Sabrina Sarvik
ISBN HARDBACK: 978-1-80559-459-8
ISBN PAPERBACK: 978-1-80559-958-6

Spirit of the Celestial Flame

In the night, a spark ignites,
Whispers from the stars invite.
Dancing shadows, hues so bright,
Embers glow with pure delight.

From the depths of silent space,
A cosmic pulse begins to race.
Winds of time, they softly trace,
Carrying dreams, they interlace.

In the heart, a flicker swells,
Guarding secrets, ancient spells.
Through the dark, the spirit dwells,
Echoes of the forge it tells.

On the wings of night it flies,
Through the veil of midnight skies.
Awakening the child that lies,
Kindling hope where silence cries.

As dawn breaks, the flame will wane,
Yet in memories, it will remain.
In every heart, it sparks again,
The spirit's gift, our endless gain.

Remnants of the Ignited Sky

Beneath the stars, whispers play,
Flickering memories, night and day.
Colors fading, the light has flown,
Echoes of warmth, forever known.

Embers dance in the cool night air,
Dreams ignited, beyond compare.
Fragments shine like scattered gold,
Stories of past, quietly told.

Ethereal Tides of the Clash

Waves crash softly on rugged stones,
Carrying tales of forgotten tones.
Whispers of battles, lost in time,
Currents that speak in silent rhyme.

Moonlit paths on the ocean swell,
Secrets of warriors, cast a spell.
Tides of history ebb and flow,
In shadows deep, the legends grow.

Celestial Shadows Unraveled

Under the veil of cosmic night,
Stars emerge, a flickering light.
Celestial tales written in glow,
Wisps of shadows, ebb and flow.

Galaxies spin in an endless dance,
Chasing whispers, lost in a trance.
A tapestry of dark and bright,
Woven together, a wondrous sight.

Sparks of the Fiery Abyss

From depths unknown, the embers rise,
Fiery whispers beneath the skies.
Restless spirits, dancing free,
Illuminating dark, fiercely.

A blaze of passion ignites the night,
Fury and warmth in gentle flight.
Each spark a story, fierce and bold,
A fiery heart, a tale retold.

Mists of the Enchanted Gale

Whispers dance through the trees,
As enchantment fills the air,
Mists weave tales on the breeze,
With secrets waiting to share.

Moonlight glimmers on the ground,
Guiding footsteps soft and light,
Where magic's pulse can be found,
In shadows cloaked by the night.

Stars above twinkle with grace,
Casting dreams upon the stream,
In this timeless, wondrous place,
Reality fades to a dream.

Silhouettes sway in delight,
Underneath the silver glow,
The world is alive tonight,
In the mists of magic's flow.

Follow the path by the sound,
Let the echoes lead your way,
In the realms of joy unbound,
Find your heart, let it stay.

Beneath the Scales of Night

The sky is draped in velvet dark,
With stars like jewels, they gleam,
Secrets hide in every spark,
Whispers float on the night's beam.

Cool winds sigh through ancient trees,
As shadows stretch and entwine,
Beneath the hush, the gentle tease,
Awakening dreams, so divine.

Creatures stir in quiet grace,
In corners where the moonlight spills,
With every flutter, every chase,
The world below laughs and thrills.

Hidden realms begin to glow,
With colors only night can paint,
In the stillness, wonders flow,
Charming hearts without restraint.

Infinite tales softly bloom,
Each waking hour bears its gift,
In the night's expansive room,
Where fantasies dance and drift.

Flickering Spirits in the Void

Glimmers brush the boundless dark,
Ethereal lights flicker near,
Spirits glide, leave no mark,
In the silence, they appear.

Echoes of laughter fill the air,
Whispers of stories untold,
As time itself pauses there,
In the embrace of the bold.

Beneath the vast celestial dome,
They weave patterns through the night,
Igniting dreams of distant home,
With every flicker, pure delight.

In the depths of silent fear,
A flicker brings a guiding star,
Illuminating paths so clear,
As every soul travels far.

Embrace the dance of light's play,
Let the spirits lead your way,
In this void where shadows blend,
Find the magic that won't end.

Wings of the Thunderous Night

Clouds converge in fury's flight,
Bolts of chaos spark the sky,
With wings that shake the cloak of night,
Storms rumble as shadows fly.

Electric whispers roam the sea,
As night's embrace starts to swell,
Nature's power wild and free,
In every drop, a tale to tell.

The winds scream through the ancient trees,
While echoes of thunder resound,
In the tempest's fierce expertise,
New beginnings can be found.

Chaos sparkles, dark and bright,
As the heavens twist and churn,
In the heart of nature's plight,
A fiery passion begins to burn.

Each heartbeat mirrors the storm,
As lightning slices through the dark,
In wildness, the world transforms,
Embracing the night's electric spark.

Luminous Spirits in the Storm's Embrace

In the heart of tempest's roar,
Luminous whispers wander and soar.
Dance on raindrops, gleam and glide,
Spirits of light, where shadows hide.

Thunder's voice calls, secrets unfold,
Mysteries wrapped in night so bold.
Electric echoes pulse through the air,
Awakening magic hidden somewhere.

Winds of change sweep the skies,
Guiding the lost with watchful eyes.
Together we rise, unbroken, whole,
Luminous spirits ignite the soul.

Storms may rage, clouds may clash,
Yet within this chaos, dreams flash.
A tapestry woven in silver threads,
Embrace of storms where courage spreads.

In the afterglow, calm will appear,
Luminous spirits, forever near.
Through the storm and into the light,
We dance on the edge of day and night.

Secrets Shrouded in Electric Mist

Beneath the veil of electric haze,
Secrets linger in twilight's gaze.
Whispers of shadows, soft and slight,
Dance with the stars, in the hush of night.

Misty figures drift and sway,
Carrying tales that fade away.
Silent echoes through the soft glow,
Unraveling riddles only they know.

Touch of the storm, a fleeting kiss,
Wrapped in wonders, we chase the bliss.
With each heartbeat, the mystery grows,
Hidden truths that the darkness knows.

Veils of wonder, wrapped in light,
Secrets shimmer, glowing bright.
Beyond the fog, we seek to find,
The whispers of fate intertwined.

In the twilight's embrace, we lose,
Dancing among the hidden clues.
For within the mist, our souls align,
Secrets await, forever divine.

Flight of the Serpent Through Midnight Haze

In the shadows where silence calls,
A serpent slithers, as night falls.
With scales aglow in moonlight's beam,
It weaves through dreams, a whispered dream.

Twisting and turning through midnight air,
Its dance is fluid, without a care.
Beneath the stars, a mystical flight,
Capturing magic, shunning the light.

Eyes of emerald, reflecting the dark,
Guided by instincts, it leaves its mark.
In the heart of the night, it plays its role,
Carving through shadows, a wandering soul.

Each curve and twist tells a tale,
Of ancient lands where the spirits prevail.
Through the haze, it moves with grace,
In the embrace of night, it finds its place.

As dawn approaches, the serpent glides,
In the wonder of night, true magic hides.
With the rising sun, its journey will cease,
But in the twilight, it dances in peace.

Ethereal Shadows Underneath Lightning's Glow

In the flicker of lightning, shadows play,
Ethereal dancers in a world of gray.
Caught in the moment where time stands still,
They weave through the dark with an intimate thrill.

The storm sings softly, a tender refrain,
As shadows spin tales of joy and pain.
Under the tumult, their secrets entwine,
Painting the sky with a touch divine.

Echoes of thunder rumble and roll,
Awakening depth within every soul.
Beneath the glow, a passage is found,
Where whispers of ages surround.

In thunder's embrace, we dare to dream,
Embracing the light, allowing the gleam.
Shadows become our guide through the night,
In the storm's wild energy, we take flight.

With each flash, the darkness reveals,
Secrets of life that the universe feels.
Underneath lightning's ethereal sheen,
We dance with shadows, forever unseen.

Beyond the Shattered Horizon

In twilight's breath, the shadows grow,
A canvas black where lost dreams flow.
Stars whisper tales of what once was,
Beyond the shattered horizon, a pause.

Waves crash down on weary shores,
Where time forgets and silence roars.
Each heartbeat echoes, a distant call,
Beneath the sky where lost hopes fall.

A path unwinds through ancient fields,
Where fate awaits, and truth yields.
In every stride, the past weaves tight,
Beyond horizons, into the night.

The sun dips low, a final glance,
Life's fleeting moments caught in dance.
With every step, we seek and find,
Beyond the shattered, a new design.

Embers glow where shadows blend,
In fractured light, hearts learn to mend.
Through the darkness, light will rise,
Beyond the shattered, hope underlies.

Dark Feathers in the Gale

Upon the winds, dark feathers glide,
Haunting echoes where secrets hide.
A whispering breeze, both soft and cold,
Promises of stories yet to be told.

Night descends, the owls cry out,
In the depths of silence, there is doubt.
Shadows stretch, their fingers entwine,
Dark feathers flicker like whispers divine.

The moonlight calls, a silver thread,
Leading the lost where angels tread.
Through tempest skies, the heart will soar,
On darkened wings, forevermore.

Echoing songs, a phantom's grace,
In the storm, we find our place.
Each gust carries a deeper lore,
Dark feathers in the gale, we explore.

With every gust, a new refrain,
In shadows' dance, we rise from pain.
A tapestry woven from night and day,
Dark feathers guide us on our way.

Chasing the Abyssal Echoes

In the depths where silence sings,
We chase the echoes of forgotten things.
Whispers of ages, a haunting sound,
In the void where shadows abound.

With each step toward the endless dark,
We seek the light, an ancient spark.
Through the currents, we dive and sway,
Chasing echoes that drift away.

Voices rise from the ocean floor,
Tales of loss and love before.
A melody wrapped in time's embrace,
Chasing the echoes, we find our place.

The waves crash hard, the world in flight,
Each echo beckons through the night.
In tangled tempests, dreams intertwine,
Chasing the abyssal, a quest divine.

Fathomless depths call to our soul,
In every heartbeat, we find our goal.
To touch the void and rise anew,
Chasing the echoes, forever true.

Flames of the Celestial Depths

From stardust born, in cosmic flames,
We spin our dreams, whispering names.
The universe trembles with our fire,
Flames of the depths, our hearts conspire.

In the vastness where shadows play,
Light ignites and guides our way.
Every spark, a tale untold,
Flames dance bright, defiance bold.

Through stellar storms and nebulae bright,
We chase the cosmos, relent to flight.
In swirling colors, our spirits rise,
Flames of the celestial, vast and wise.

Each moment burns, a fleeting glow,
In the tapestry of night, we flow.
The universe holds, in its gentle sweep,
Flames of the depths, our secrets keep.

As suns align and destinies weave,
In cosmic flames, we dare to believe.
A journey endless, our hearts will dance,
Flames of the celestial, in eternal trance.

Twilight's Caress on Sulfurous Winds

As daylight fades, a hush descends,
Soft whispers ride on tempest's breath,
The sky adorned with fiery bends,
Embrace the dusk, defy the death.

Crimson streaks on horizon's line,
Sulfurous winds weave tales of old,
Each gust a dance, a secret sign,
Nature's secrets, fiercely bold.

Among the shadows, echoes stir,
Twilight's kiss on every face,
The world unravels, soft and pure,
In fleeting moments, time finds grace.

Oft in the stillness, hearts will race,
For storms that brew in parting light,
And memories of that sweet embrace,
Caught in a whirlwind, day to night.

Echoing Flames in a Silent Sky

Silent ashes float on high,
Among the stars, they drift and play,
Echoes alive in the midnight sky,
Whispers of love, in shadows, stay.

Flames that flicker, dance and glow,
Casting warmth on cold, pale earth,
Stories of long-lost tales flow,
In every spark, a moment's birth.

Time stands still as embers reign,
A silent vow in twilight's grace,
Each flame a pulse, a sweet refrain,
In the distance, fate finds its place.

Under the cover of night so deep,
Dreams ignite, and hope shines bright,
In every heartbeat, secrets keep,
Yearning for dawn, our guiding light.

Shimmering Veils in the Storm's Eye

Veils of silver, shadows dance,
In the storm's heart, chaos sings,
Soft light breaks through a fleeting chance,
A glimpse of peace that chaos brings.

Raindrops blend in currents wild,
Nature's rhythm, fierce and free,
Within the tempest, beauty's child,
Whirls in circles, endlessly.

Winds that howl and skies that weep,
Each droplet tells a tale anew,
Through storms we tread, our spirits leap,
Finding solace, breaking through.

In shimmering veils, we see the light,
The eye of calm amidst the fray,
A promise held in the darkest night,
Guiding us home when skies turn gray.

Nightfall's Lament Under His Majesty

Beneath the stars, the shadows creep,
Nightfall cloaks the world below,
In silence deep, where secrets sleep,
His majesty moves with regal flow.

Lost in whispers, time slows down,
The moonlit path unfolds ahead,
In every corner, night's soft crown,
An embrace to guide the spirit led.

Each heartbeat echoes with the night,
As dreams emerge from dusky places,
In twilight's hush, we seek the light,
Beneath the gaze of ancient faces.

Lament for those who lost their way,
In shadows thick, the lost do roam,
Yet under stars, hope finds a ray,
With nightfall's grace, we'll find our home.

Shard of the Moonlit Force

In the stillness, whispers rise,
A glow where silence lies,
Crystals spark in hidden streams,
Casting light on secret dreams.

Through the night, the shadows play,
Dancing softly, lost in sway,
Each glimmer pierces darkened veils,
Carrying echoes of old tales.

Time drips slow like melting wax,
Embers hold what memory lacks,
Fragmented beams, a lover's sigh,
Connected still, though worlds deny.

Beneath the watchful, tranquil skies,
Shards of silver, love's reprise,
Weaving magic in the air,
Binding hearts with threads of care.

In this realm, where dreams unfold,
Each secret light, a story told,
A shard of force from moonlit birth,
Illuminates our fragile worth.

Tides of Celestial Twilight

In twilight's arms, the stars awake,
Softly weaving what tides make,
With every pulse, the heavens sigh,
As visions flow from sea to sky.

Whispers travel on night's breeze,
Carried far past ancient trees,
Each wave a thought, a fleeting wish,
Carved in depths where silence swish.

The horizon glimmers with lost fate,
As dreams emerge, hesitate,
Endless echoes of things once known,
In celestial hues, we are shown.

Dance of shadows, ebb and flow,
Guides us through the twilight glow,
Each moment vast as the endless sea,
Unraveled threads of destiny.

In depths of night, we rise anew,
Heeding whispers, feeling true,
Tides of wonder, hearts entwined,
Chasing stardust, we are blind.

The Gloom of Forgotten Realms

In realms forgotten, shadows creep,
Veils of gloom, secrets keep,
Whispers echo through the dust,
Breath of time, a fragile trust.

Landscapes bend in twilight's grasp,
Lost in dreams, we yearn to clasp,
Each turn of fate, a tale erased,
In shadowed corners, hope is chased.

Silent echoes of past despair,
Haunting souls in stillness stare,
Yet in the dark, a flicker glows,
Where light persists, and courage grows.

Through hollow halls of ancient stone,
Memories whisper, we are not alone,
In forgotten realms, hearts may mend,
Finding solace with every bend.

The gloom may thicken, shadows blight,
Yet even dusk yields to dawn's light,
In realms of sorrow, strength will bloom,
Risen high from shadows of gloom.

Tempest of Shadowed Hopes

In the heart of storms, we tremble,
Winds of doubt and dreams assemble,
Veiled intentions twist and rush,
In the tempest, voices hush.

Whirling clouds of lost desires,
Embers flicker, stoked by fires,
Each hope a shard, caught mid-flight,
Piercing through the shroud of night.

Fate entwined in shadows' fold,
Weathered hearts, both bright and bold,
Chasing whispers through the gale,
In tempests fierce, we will not fail.

From chaos blooms an inner strength,
Resilience found in every length,
In stormy seas, we find our way,
Guided by the light of day.

So let the tempest howl and scream,
For in the dark, we still will dream,
In shadowed hopes, we rise again,
Defying storms, our hearts remain.

Fragments of Celestial Dreams

Stars whisper softly in the night,
Wishes take flight, like birds in sight.
Moonbeams dance on a silver stream,
In the silence, we chase our dream.

Clouds drift softly, a gentle sigh,
Cradling visions that float and fly.
In the darkness, a light appears,
Binding our hopes, calming our fears.

Comets streak across the vast expanse,
Every glance a fleeting chance.
Constellations weave stories bright,
Guiding our hearts through endless night.

Galaxies swirl in an endless hue,
In the cosmos, our spirits accrue.
Fragments of joy in the stellar dance,
In every twinkle, a whispered chance.

A lullaby sung by the infinite space,
Filling our souls with its warm embrace.
We gather the pieces, both near and far,
In the realm of dreams, we are the stars.

Secrets of the Fiery Night

Embers flicker in the darkened sky,
Whispers of flames that dance and fly.
Beneath the moon, shadows intertwine,
As the secrets of fire brightly shine.

Crimson clouds engulf the glade,
Each heartbeat matched with the blade.
The wind carries tales of ancient lore,
Echoing softly forevermore.

Stars twinkle like gems, fierce and bold,
Illuminating secrets of old.
Night unfurls its tapestry wide,
As the shadows embrace the tide.

Here in the stillness, the magic swells,
In every flicker, a story dwells.
The fiery night speaks to the soul,
Guiding us gently toward our goal.

As dawn approaches, the flames grow dim,
Yet the night's secrets will never slim.
In memory's grace, the fiery light,
Lives on, enduring through every night.

Echoes from the Abyss

Deep in the dark, where shadows creep,
Echoes of lost souls stir from sleep.
Whispers of longing, a haunting call,
From the depth of the abyss, we fall.

Waves crash softly against the stone,
Carrying sorrow, endlessly blown.
Secrets concealed where the light can't tread,
In the depths where the whispers are fed.

Ghostly apparitions float and sway,
Reminders of dreams that faded away.
With every heartbeat, the darkness sighs,
As echoes resound beneath the skies.

Time stands still in this haunted space,
Loss and desire find their place.
Yet in the shadows, a flicker glows,
Hope rises where the dark wind blows.

From the abyss, we forge our path,
Wrestling with fear, enduring the wrath.
In the silence, the echoes remain,
A testament of both joy and pain.

In the Wake of the Dragon's Breath

In the shadows of mountains high,
Legends linger where dragons fly.
Fires burn bright with a fierce delight,
As their breath ignites the starry night.

Scales shimmer in the moon's soft light,
Guardians of dreams taking flight.
Tales of old, etched in the air,
In their presence, we lose our care.

The earth trembles beneath their might,
Awakening echoes of ancient fight.
Through valleys deep, their spirits roam,
In the fire's glow, we find our home.

Claws carve paths through wide-open skies,
As hearts beat strong, and courage flies.
In the wake of their breath, we feel alive,
With fervent hopes, we begin to thrive.

Every heartbeat, a promise kept,
In dreams of flight, our worries swept.
Dragons soar, and our spirits blend,
In their fiery wake, we find our end.

Echoes of a Shattered Oath

In shadows where whispers dwell,
Promises lost, a broken spell.
Footsteps trail in silence deep,
Echoes of trust we cannot keep.

Hearts heavy with unshed tears,
Haunted by forgotten years.
Vows once bright, now fade from sight,
Left to linger in the night.

The winds carry tales of woe,
Secrets bound in undertow.
From ashes of love, the ghosts rise,
In the dark, they wear disguise.

With each breath, the pain revives,
A reminder of shattered lives.
Yet in the shards, there's strength to find,
A path anew, for the heart and mind.

Though trust may break and bonds decay,
Hope flickers, won't fade away.
In the echoes of past regret,
A chance to heal, we won't forget.

Illuminated Secrets of the Twilight

Beneath the veil of twilight's grace,
Hidden dreams in shadowed space.
Whispers dance on the cool night air,
Secrets linger, light and rare.

Stars awaken, a distant choir,
Filling hearts with timeless fire.
Glimmers of truth in twilight's glow,
Guide us where we yearn to go.

Shadows stretch, the world transforms,
Mysteries in celestial forms.
The night reveals what day may hide,
In this stillness, we confide.

With each heartbeat, the cosmos sighs,
Reflections in the endless skies.
Infinite tales in soft embrace,
Breathe life into this sacred space.

Illuminated paths await,
Underneath the stars' quiet fate.
In the twilight, we find release,
A fleeting moment, a sense of peace.

The Spirit's Celestial Outcry

From heights where the ancients soar,
The spirit calls, forevermore.
In winds that sing of distant lands,
Wisdom flows through unseen hands.

Stars align with the heart's true plea,
An echo of all that's meant to be.
In the void where silence reigns,
A cry of hope amidst the pains.

Galaxies weave through the night's embrace,
Whispered truths in a sacred space.
From depths of darkness, light may rise,
The spirit's song, a cosmic surprise.

As comets blaze across the sphere,
The spirit's voice is crystal clear.
Listen closely, feel the breath,
For in this echo, lies no death.

In every star, a story bold,
Of journeys new and worlds of old.
The spirit dances, wild and free,
In the celestial tapestry.

Dance of Flickering Embers

In the hearth, where warmth ignites,
Flickering embers play with lights.
Stories told in crackling flair,
Magic weaves a tapestry rare.

As shadows sway, the night unfolds,
Whispers of passion through the cold.
Each spark a vision, bright and bold,
In the dance where souls are sold.

The air is thick with memories past,
Time suspended, moments cast.
With every glow, a heartbeat shared,
In the warmth, we are ensnared.

Embers rise, a fleeting flight,
Together we blaze into the night.
Lost in the rhythm, we find our song,
In this dance, we all belong.

When morning comes, the fire wanes,
Yet in our hearts, the warmth remains.
Flickering embers, a whispered kiss,
In the silence, we find our bliss.

Lurking in the Ashen Light

In shadows deep where whispers sigh,
The ashen light begins to cry.
Ghostly figures weave through time,
Their secrets lost, a silent rhyme.

The echoes dance on dusty floors,
Remnants of what was before.
Flickering flames of memories fade,
As dreams succumb to night's cascade.

A flicker bright, a fleeting spark,
Illuminates the lingering dark.
Yet hope remains, a stubborn flame,
In ashen light, we speak its name.

The world outside, a distant hum,
While shadows play and silence drums.
Lurking still beneath the guise,
The heart's own truths can never die.

Radiance of Lost Oaths

In twilight's glow, the vows once sworn,
Lie tangled now, in silence torn.
The echo soft of promises made,
In whispers lost, as dreams do fade.

Beneath the stars, we danced so bright,
Our hearts ablaze, each kiss a light.
Yet with the dawn, the shadows creep,
And in their grasp, our memories sleep.

We carved our names in fleeting air,
With laughter sweet, and tender care.
Yet time, a thief, with quiet stealth,
Takes all the warmth, leaves naught but wealth.

In empty rooms where echoes fill,
The radiance dims, a bittersweet thrill.
Still linger close, those ghosts of old,
Their tales of love, forever told.

Glimmers in the Tempest

The tempest roars with fury bright,
Yet glimmers shine amidst the night.
Flickering stars, a distant desire,
Guide lost souls through wind and fire.

In chaos swirls, where shadows play,
Hope's fragile spark won't fade away.
For every scream, a whispered prayer,
In the storm's heart, we learn to care.

Waves crash down like thunder's might,
Yet in the dark, there's still the light.
Each heartbeat drums a steady tune,
A call to dance beneath the moon.

Though storms may rage and darkness bite,
In every trial, there's strength in sight.
Together we stand, united and brave,
For glimmers shine even in the grave.

The Serpent's Veil

Beneath the cloak of emerald green,
A serpent coils, sleek and keen.
With eyes aglow, it silently waits,
In whispered lore, it captivates.

The secrets held within its gaze,
Entwine the heart in mystic haze.
Each scale a story, woven tight,
Bound in shadows, kissed by light.

To tread too close is to embrace,
The dance of fate, a fleeting grace.
As twilight falls, the veil unfurls,
In silence deep, the world twirls.

A labyrinth spun of dreams and fears,
Where all that glitters may bring tears.
Yet seek the truth within the dark,
For wisdom lies in every mark.

Incandescence of the Night's Breath

Beneath the stars, whispers dance slow,
Moonlight weaves tales in silver glow.
Dreams unfurl like blossoms in flight,
Embracing the magic of the night.

Shadows sway with secrets untold,
Time's gentle pulse, a rhythm bold.
In quietude, hearts find their song,
Where darkness cradles, we all belong.

A chill in the air, tender and sweet,
Echoes of laughter, soft and discrete.
Night's breath lingers, a serene caress,
Wrapped in the warmth of sweet finesse.

Stars flicker bright, as if to share,
Wishes that float like feathers in air.
Each moment cherished, a glimmering thread,
Weaving our hopes where dreams are bred.

Incandescent glow, a beacon of light,
Guiding the lost through the velvet night.
In every heartbeat, a story's spun,
In the night's breath, we are all one.

Celestial Fragments in Gloomy Serenity

In quietude, the stars collide,
Fragments of light in shadows glide.
A canvas of black, with specks of gold,
Whispers of worlds, waiting to be told.

Surrounded by silence, peace takes flight,
Echoes of cosmos, soft as the night.
Darkness, a blanket, soothing and deep,
Cradling dreams as the universe sleeps.

Clouds drift above, painting the sky,
Carrying secrets as they float by.
Each raindrop a promise, a tear from the light,
Reflecting the beauty hidden from sight.

In this gloom, serenity reigns,
Moments of wonder, breaking the chains.
Each piece of the puzzle, a sight to behold,
In celestial fragments, the story unfolds.

Fleeting yet timeless, the cosmos observes,
Guiding each heart with the love it deserves.
In gloomy serenity, we find our way,
Embracing the fragments of night and day.

Aurora's Touch on the Stormy Horizon

Storm clouds gather, a tempest brews,
In the distance, the night sky hues.
A flicker of light breaks through the gray,
Aurora's touch, igniting the day.

Colors collide in a vibrant dance,
Nature's palette, a fleeting chance.
The storm whispers soft, a melody rare,
Wraps the horizon in radiance fair.

As lightning flashes, shadows entwine,
Under the gaze of a sky so divine.
Each heartbeat echoes the pulse of the storm,
Holding the promise of warmth to transform.

Splashes of emerald, scarlet, and gold,
Paint the tempest, a sight to behold.
Through chaos and thunder, hope shines bright,
For even in storms, emerges the light.

With every new dawn, the dark will recede,
Nature awakens, fulfilling the need.
Aurora's caress on the horizon's crest,
Brings forth the beauty, a world at rest.

Fables Carved in the Breath of Dragons

In whispered tales, the dragons dwell,
Guardians of secrets, casting their spell.
Fables of fire and shadows take flight,
Echoes of wisdom in the deep night.

Scales that shimmer, a tempest in flight,
Breathe life into stories, illuminating the night.
Through the ages, their legends have soared,
In the pulse of the earth, their magic adored.

From mountains high to valleys below,
Fables of courage awaken the glow.
Each breath, a saga, a moment, a dream,
Carved in the twilight, their essence a beam.

With wings unfurling, they dance in the skies,
Living library, where history lies.
In their eyes, the cosmos and time intertwine,
Breath of the dragons, in heartbeats divine.

Through echoes of ages, adventures unfold,
In the tales of the brave, the timid, the bold.
Fables carved gently in the stillness of night,
Guardians of dreams, igniting our light.

Whispers of the Celestial Flame

In the dusk where shadows creep,
A flicker stirs from dreams so deep.
Stars glimmer, tales unfold,
In whispers soft, secrets told.

Fireflies flit in night's embrace,
Illuminating a hidden space.
Fires of old ignite the sky,
In hush of night, the spirits fly.

Glimmers dance on waves of thought,
In every spark, the universe caught.
Celestial songs echo clear,
In the silence, we draw near.

With every breath, the cosmos sighs,
In the heart of night, magic lies.
A melody of dreams ignites,
In the glow of distant lights.

Hold close the warmth of ancient flames,
As stardust whispers forgotten names.
In the dark, let shadows play,
Guiding souls along the way.

The Eclipsed Dance of Light

In twilight's hush, a shimmer brews,
Moonlight casts an argent muse.
Shadows stretch, the world awaits,
As daylight fades, the night elates.

Stars align in silent grace,
Time slows down, a sweet embrace.
Eclipsed in stillness, hearts unite,
To dance beneath the soft moonlight.

Whispers of the night entwine,
With every beat, the stars align.
A ballet of the dark and bright,
In the cosmos, infinite flight.

Glimmers fade, yet hope remains,
In every shadow, joy sustains.
A cycle turning, light and shade,
In the universe, dreams are laid.

As dawn approaches, gently bright,
We bid adieu to the dance of night.
With every heartbeat, life ignites,
In the embrace of fading lights.

Twisted Echoes of Thunder

In the heart of the storm's fierce roar,
Nature speaks with a voice of lore.
Lightning dances, bold and wild,
Echoes call, the tempest's child.

Clouds collide in a furious claim,
Each crack a spark, stoking the flame.
In the chaos, truth resounds,
In twisted echoes, power abounds.

Raindrops fall like whispered prayers,
Woven tales in the heavy airs.
A symphony where silence ends,
In the clash, the spirit mends.

From the dark, a vision calls,
As nature's fury breaks down walls.
In the storm's heart, the world's awake,
In trembling earth, our fears we shake.

When thunder fades, peace finds its way,
In the stillness, dreams hold sway.
What was chaos becomes the calm,
In echoes lost, we find our balm.

Vestiges of the Celestial Realm

Underneath the starry dome,
Echoes of the past call us home.
Galaxies whisper tales of old,
In shadows cast, their secrets unfold.

Flickers of light weave through the air,
Guiding souls with tender care.
Every twinkle a memory bright,
In the expanse of the velvet night.

Dimensions blur in cosmic grace,
Lost in the vastness, we find our place.
Time unfolds like an ancient scroll,
In the heart of the universe, we feel whole.

Dreamers drift on astral waves,
In the silence, the cosmos saves.
A journey through realms, both near and far,
Where every heartbeat aligns with a star.

Bearing witness to the grand design,
In every breath, a spark divine.
The vestiges of all that's real,
In the dance of light, we learn to heal.

Wings of the Enigmatic Night

Beneath a shroud of velvet skies,
The whispers weave a tale untold.
Stars flicker with their ancient sighs,
As shadows dance and secrets unfold.

A silver moon with gentle light,
Guides wanderers lost in their dreams.
Silence blankets the restless night,
While mystery stirs in silent streams.

The nightingale sings soft and low,
Her voice a soothing, haunting sound.
Every heartbeat begins to flow,
With the mystique that wraps around.

Through tangled branches, shadows play,
Chasing secrets, they slip away.
The horizon blushes with the dawn,
As the enigmatic wings are drawn.

In flight, they soar on whispered gales,
Exploring worlds where wonder dwells.
Night's embrace, a tender sigh,
In the dark, our spirits fly.

Glistening Shadows on the Edge

Along the cliff where night meets day,
Glistening shadows begin to sway.
The wind whispers of tales unbound,
While echoes of light dance all around.

The sea reflects the starlit glow,
Each wave a story from long ago.
Mysteries linger just out of sight,
Guarded by the secrets of night.

Crimson hues stain the sky's embrace,
As twilight brushes the world's face.
Silhouettes flicker with each new breeze,
Painting dreams among the trees.

A world defined by dusk's allure,
Where shadows hold their magic pure.
Glistening edges softly blend,
In the twilight that never ends.

With each heartbeat, the night grows near,
As silence wraps all we hold dear.
In this embrace of shadowed light,
We find our place in the vast night.

Gleaming Beneath the Ruined Skies

Beneath the ruins of once-proud dreams,
A glimmer stirs and softly gleams.
Old stone remembers stories bright,
Held within the heart of night.

Through cracks and crevices, life does creep,
Whispers of hope through silence seep.
Gleaming flowers in shadows bloom,
Defying ashes, igniting gloom.

Rays of sunlight, a gentle caress,
Awakening the weary to bless.
In the ruins, life finds a way,
A testament to every day.

So we gather beneath the skies,
Learning from rubble where wisdom lies.
With every breath, we rise anew,
Gleaming brighter in vibrant hue.

The past may crumble, the skies may gray,
Yet from the ashes, we find our way.
United, we stand in the face of fate,
Gleaming beneath the ruins' weight.

Echoes of Forgotten Thunder

In the distance, a rumble calls,
Echoes of thunder from ancient halls.
Memories stir in the cool evening air,
Whispers of storms, beckoning everywhere.

Clouds gather, weaving tales of old,
Of battles fought and legends bold.
Every crackle, a ghostly sigh,
Of dreams once chased, now passing by.

The earth trembles to the rhythmic beat,
Of time's embrace beneath our feet.
With every storm, we learn, we grow,
In the pulse of thunder, wisdom flows.

Lightning flashes, illuminating night,
As shadows blend in the fierce light.
Each roar stirs a fire within,
Fueling the courage to start again.

Through echoes shared in the twilight's glow,
We find strength in the thunder's flow.
A symphony born of nature's grace,
Echoes of thunder, time's embrace.

Within the Searing Mist

In shadows deep, the mists arise,
Veiling the world in mystery's guise.
Whispers echo in the dampened air,
A haunting chill, an unseen stare.

Through the fog, a figure glides,
With eyes aglow, where secrets hide.
Each step reveals a tale untold,
In the shrouded realm, both brave and bold.

The silence thick, the heartbeat loud,
Amongst the wisps, a ghostly crowd.
Embers flicker in the hidden gloom,
Guiding the lost to destiny's bloom.

With every breath, the mist takes form,
In the haze, where shadows swarm.
A dance of fate, a lure of time,
Each fleeting moment draped in rhyme.

So venture forth in searing mist,
Embrace the tale that can't be missed.
For in the fog, the truth ignites,
And guides the soul through endless nights.

The Breath of the Celestial Beast

In twilight's grasp, a power stirs,
The cosmos hums, as silence blurs.
With wings aflame, the stars align,
To cradle dreams with a breath divine.

From silver clouds, the beast takes flight,
A guardian cloaked in shimmering light.
With every roar, the heavens quake,
Creating worlds, the night awakes.

Its breath, a whisper, celestial song,
Harmonious symphonies, grand and strong.
Painting hues across the night sky,
As constellations begin to sigh.

Through cosmic seas, a voyage unfolds,
As stories ancient, the starlight holds.
In its embrace, the universe spins,
An everlasting dance, where hope begins.

So heed the call of the celestial beast,
In its embrace, fears are released.
For with each breath, the world renews,
Awakening dreams, in cosmic hues.

Mists of Ancient Whispers

In shadows cast by ancient trees,
The mists arise, a gentle tease.
Whispers float on the cool, crisp air,
Echoes of wisdom, hidden with care.

The forest breathes, alive with lore,
Each sighing breeze opens a door.
To tales of yore, where spirits tread,
In hallowed ground, where dreams are fed.

From roots entwined in secrets deep,
The voices stir from their slumbered sleep.
They beckon forth, with promises sweet,
To guide the wanderers, lost on their feet.

Through winding paths and glades serene,
The mists unveil what once had been.
Like silken threads of forgotten times,
They weave together, the old and the prime.

So listen close, in the morning dew,
For in the mists, wisdom flows anew.
Embrace the whispers, let them ignite,
A journey through darkness, toward the light.

Adrift in the Celestial Echo

In the void where silence reigns,
Drifts a soul with ancient pains.
Starbound echoes lace the air,
In cosmic dreams, they weave a snare.

A tapestry of light unfolds,
Revealing tales that time enfolds.
Each note resounds, a siren's call,
Luring the heart to rise and fall.

Galaxies spin in a balletic waltz,
As cosmic rhythms pen our faults.
With every pulse, the universe sighs,
Whispers of love in the starry skies.

Through realms unknown, the spirit roams,
In search of truths, in celestial homes.
Lost in echoes, yet never alone,
In every heartbeat, the cosmos is known.

So drift away, in the boundless sea,
Where echoes dance, and souls are free.
For in the vastness, we find our place,
Adrift in echoes, we embrace grace.

Fragments of Light in a Whirling Storm

In the heart of chaos, bright glimmers fade,
Whispers of hope beneath the tempest's cascade.
Fleeting moments caught in the swirling night,
Fragments of joy, like stars slipping from sight.

Clouds weave their tapestry, dark tales unfold,
A symphony wild, both bitter and bold.
Yet through the maelstrom, a flicker ignites,
Guiding lost souls toward the softest of lights.

Rains pelt the earth with a furious grace,
Yet shadows retreat from the warmth we embrace.
In the depths of storms, we discover our might,
Finding our solace, our fragments of light.

Amidst fierce winds and the echoes of fear,
A dance of resilience brings faces so dear.
We rise through the squall, with spirits unchained,
In fragments of light, true courage proclaimed.

So let the storm howl, let the tempest roar,
For we are the lanterns, forever we soar.
With each crack of thunder, our hearts learn to sing,
In fragments of light, our liberation takes wing.

A Serenade of Shadows and Sparks

In the twilight hour, shadows begin to weave,
A soft serenade, for those who believe.
Sparks dance in silence, glowing with grace,
Telling a story with each flickering trace.

Moonlight's embrace bathes darkness in gold,
While secrets of night start to gently unfold.
Whispers of history echo through trees,
As shadows collide with the soft evening breeze.

In this realm of twilight, both gentle and stark,
Every step we take leaves a luminous mark.
A canvas of dreams, painted with sighs,
As moments ignited in darkness arise.

The melody deepens, as stars join the song,
Each shadow and spark knows where they belong.
Together they twirl in a mystical dance,
In the serenade's magic, we find our romance.

So let us embrace the twilight's sweet call,
Where shadows and sparks waltz, enchanting us all.
In the stillness of night, with hearts open wide,
We find our own rhythm, we dance side by side.

Dreams Wrapped in Celestial Thunder

Beneath the vast heavens, dreams softly bloom,
Wrapped in the echoes of thunderous gloom.
A tempest of wishes, both wild and rare,
Whispers of fate ripple through the air.

Stars in their glory, like lanterns aglow,
Guide the lost dreams on a journey they go.
Each flash of lightning reveals hidden paths,
Where courage ignites amidst nature's loud wrath.

In the chaos of night, hope can ignite,
Carving out spaces where shadows take flight.
Celestial wonders blanket the space,
Awakening visions with infinite grace.

Let the storm rage, for it's in the strife,
That dreams find their power, that dreams find their life.
In thunder's embrace, our spirits take wing,
As we dance with the heavens, in freedom we sing.

For dreams wrapped in thunder shall never be tamed,
Each pulse of the cosmos, our hearts are framed.
In the vastness above, let our wishes take form,
As we gather our dreams amidst celestial storm.

The Dance of Dusk and Draconic Echoes

As dusk paints the skies with a fiery hue,
Draconic whispers bring tales old yet new.
Wings stretch out wide, brushing against night,
In the dance of shadows, there's magic and fright.

Emerald glimmers in the fading light,
Scales shimmering softly, a wondrous sight.
Ancient stories echo from mountain and vale,
In the twilight's embrace, we ride on their trail.

Fire and flight mingle with stars overhead,
In the dance of dusk, where legends are bred.
Each beat of the wings brings forth a new song,
A melody woven where we all belong.

From shadows we rise, with spirits unbound,
In draconic echoes, the lost can be found.
Heartbeats align with the pulse of the earth,
United in rhythm, we celebrate birth.

So let the dusk shimmer, let the dragons soar,
For in their embrace, we discover much more.
The dance never ends, it's a cycle of light,
In dusks and in echoes, our souls take flight.

Shadows Whisper in the Storm

In the depth of night, they creep,
Silent whispers, secrets keep,
Raindrops tap on windowpane,
Nature's call, a soft refrain.

Clouds collide in a mournful song,
Echoes linger, deep and strong,
Lightning cracks, a fleeting light,
Shadows dance, then take to flight.

Thunder rumbles, bass so deep,
While the world in silence weeps,
Flickering candles start to fade,
In the storm, our fears displayed.

Through the tempest, a voice rings clear,
Whispers urging us to steer,
Guided by the shadows' grace,
In this dark, we find our place.

As the storm begins to wane,
Nature's tears, like softest rain,
In the aftermath, we stand tall,
Listening to the shadows' call.

Flickering Echoes of Dusk

The sun dips low, a final bow,
Colors blend, like whispered vow,
Fingers of twilight gently trace,
Painting night with soft embrace.

Stars begin to pierce the gloom,
Nighttime blooms, dispelling doom,
Each flicker tells a timeless tale,
Echoes dance upon the pale.

Crickets sing their evening tune,
Underneath the watchful moon,
While shadows weave a silken seam,
Life's a gentle, fading dream.

In the hush, we start to pause,
Lost in thought, without a cause,
Dusk invites the heart to roam,
In the dusk, we find our home.

As darkness wraps its velvet cloak,
Whispers shared, no need for spoke,
Flickering echoes, soft and bright,
Guide us gently into night.

Veil of Midnight Flames

In the woodland, shadows rise,
Midnight whispers, ancient cries,
Flames flicker, casting light,
Veils of magic in the night.

Each ember tells a tale long lost,
Of love and dreams, no matter the cost,
Ghostly figures dance and sway,
In the heart, they choose to stay.

The air thick with secrets old,
Stories of the brave and bold,
Through the flames, visions gleam,
A tapestry of hope and dream.

Fingers reach to touch the fire,
Hearts ignited by desire,
Veil of night, a cloak profound,
In the darkness, truths are found.

When the dawn begins to break,
And the world begins to wake,
We carry forth the warmth and light,
From the veil of midnight's flight.

Secrets of the Serpent's Dance

In the shadows where no light,
Serpents slither, quiet, slight,
Their movements weave a mystic flow,
Secrets held beneath the glow.

Each twist and turn, an ancient rite,
In the dark, they own the night,
Wisdom hidden, tales unfold,
Guardians of the stories told.

With scales that shimmer, secrets shine,
In their dance, the world aligns,
Rhythms pulse, a heartbeat's call,
Inviting all to heed the thrall.

As they weave through woods and glen,
Life's great circle starts again,
Whispered truths that bind the earth,
In their movement lies rebirth.

So heed the dance, embrace the sound,
In the serpent's twist, we're found,
Turn the key, unlock the trance,
Discover life in each advance.

Shadows Dance in Celestial Currents

In the night, shadows swirl,
Celestial lights softly twirl.
Stars awaken, secrets shared,
In the silence, dreams are bared.

Glimmers flicker, life takes flight,
Guided by the silver light.
Whispers echo through the void,
Crafting worlds yet to be enjoyed.

Galaxies whisper, tales unfold,
Stories woven, a dance of old.
Each hue and tone, a gentle sigh,
In this vastness, we learn to fly.

Cosmic breezes, gently sway,
Carrying hopes along the way.
In the quiet, hearts align,
As the universe, we redefine.

Whispers of the Thunderous Sky

Beneath the clouds, a rumble spreads,
Nature speaks where silence treads.
Lightning splits the darkened air,
Whispers echo, shadows stare.

Raindrops drum on rooftops low,
A symphony of undertow.
Each heartbeat sounds with thunder's call,
In this moment, we're all enthralled.

Storm's embrace, both fierce and sweet,
Nature's power, raw and neat.
In chaos, beauty finds its way,
As night unfolds into the day.

Clouds collide, a dance of might,
Illuminating the darkest night.
In the tempest, we find grace,
Whispers linger, a warm embrace.

Flickering Echoes of Ancient Fire

In the hearth, the embers glow,
Stories etched in flickered flow.
Ancient tales of love and strife,
Carved in time, a dance of life.

Warmth surrounds, a comforting light,
Guiding shadows through the night.
Flickering whispers, a call to dream,
In every spark, a silent scream.

Echoes bounce off weathered walls,
Carrying voices, a siren's calls.
From ashes rise a spirit bold,
In fiery depths, legends told.

The flame dances, reciting lore,
Kindling hearts forevermore.
In the glow, we find our way,
Guided by the fire's display.

Veils of Darkness in a Tempest's Grasp

Veils of night, shrouded in fear,
Tempest whispers, drawing near.
Gales collide with silent might,
Crafting shadows, swallowing light.

Darkness lingers, weaving fate,
Every heartbeat echoes, weight.
Inside this storm, courage grows,
As hope flickers, still it glows.

Clouds stretch wide, a daunting veil,
Yet in the dark, we shall not fail.
For in the tempest, strength is born,
Rising strong with each new dawn.

Grit and will, we lift our gaze,
Through swirling winds, we seek our ways.
In every shadow, light exists,
Guiding us through twilight's mist.

Flickers of the Twilit Skies

In twilight hues the whispers play,
Between the stars where shadows sway,
Flickers dance on the cusp of night,
Cradled in the twilight's light.

The moon begins her gentle rise,
Casting dreams from silver skies,
And turning whispers into song,
Where every heart can feel they belong.

Fingers painting skies so deep,
Secrets held that they will keep,
Golden rays and violet streams,
Weaving tales of softest dreams.

As time unwinds its precious thread,
Soft winds carry words unsaid,
Each flicker tells a story true,
Under skies of fading blue.

In every breath a moment lingers,
As if touched by unseen fingers,
The twilight speaks in colors bright,
Flickers of the coming night.

Shadows Enkindled by Storms

Beneath the clouds, a restless roar,
As shadows dance on the ocean's floor,
Enkindled by the thunder's beat,
A symphony of dark and sweet.

Lightning flashes, bright and bold,
Stories of the storm unfold,
Deep within the tempest's heart,
Is where the shadows find their art.

Winds howl across the barren ground,
A haunting melody profound,
With every gust, a tale is spun,
Of battles lost and victories won.

The skies weep, but there's a grace,
In nature's fierce and wild embrace,
For in the chaos, life takes form,
From shadows enkindled by the storm.

As rain cascades and rivers swell,
Each drop a wish, a whispered spell,
In the darkness, a fiery glow,
Where shadows dance, and spirits flow.

Secrets in the Tempest's Grasp

Amidst the storm's fierce, wild embrace,
Secrets churn in the tempest's race,
Winds carry whispers of the past,
In the shadows, memories cast.

Each thunderclap a voice reborn,
Echoing through the night, forlorn,
The raindrops fall as sacred signs,
In chaotic rhythms, truth aligns.

Lightning reveals what's long been hid,
Unveiling tales the night had bid,
In tempest's hold, the soul ignites,
Awakening dreams in stormy nights.

The heart of nature beats so loud,
Bursting forth like a tempest's crowd,
Secrets woven in every gust,
In the storm, we place our trust.

As calm descends, and silence takes,
Whispers linger in the wakes,
What once was lost, now ever near,
In secrets held, we find our cheer.

Dreams Wreathed in Emberlight

In the glow of embers bright,
Dreams take flight in the hush of night,
Wreathed in warmth, they softly gleam,
Carried by a wistful dream.

Flickering flames, soft shadows play,
Guiding wishes along their way,
With every spark a hope ignites,
In the stillness of gentle nights.

From ashes rise the tales of old,
Whispers of love and hearts of gold,
Each crackle sings of what can be,
In the emberlight, we are free.

As morning breaks, shadows give way,
To sunlit paths where dreams can stay,
Yet still we hold the warmth inside,
Where emberlight and dreams abide.

In glowing coals, our stories rest,
In every heartbeat, every quest,
Dreams wreathed in emberlight will soar,
Forever cherished, forever more.

Whispers of Fiery Secrets

In shadows deep, the embers glow,
Whispers of secrets, soft and low.
Each flicker tells a tale untold,
Of passions burned and dreams of gold.

Beneath the night, where silence reigns,
The heat of flames, the pulse of veins.
In every spark, a memory wakes,
Of love's embrace and heartache's aches.

Dancing hues in twilight's grasp,
Warmth and longing, a tender clasp.
Through smoke and ash, the truth will seep,
In fiery whispers, secrets keep.

With every blaze, a lesson learned,
In flickering flames, desires burned.
A symphony of light and dark,
In fiery whispers, we leave our mark.

So let them burn, our hidden truth,
In fiery secrets, found in youth.
For every spark, a dream to chase,
In whispers soft, we find our place.

Enigmatic Flames on the Horizon

Beyond the dawn, the embers rise,
Enigmas wrapped in sunrise skies.
Flames dance wild to a silent tune,
As daybreak turns the night to ruin.

Mist caresses the shimmering light,
Painting tales with colors bright.
The horizon glows with secrets frail,
A story whispered on the gale.

Each flicker holds a promise neat,
Of journeys taken on golden feet.
Together we chase the glowing hue,
In flames entwined, just me and you.

As shadows fade to certainty,
We ignite paths for all to see.
With every blaze, the heart beat grows,
In enigmatic flames, love overflows.

From ashes new, our hope ascends,
In every heart, the fire mends.
With vibrant echoes of dawn's embrace,
We blaze our trails, our sacred space.

Celestial Veils in Twilight

Beneath the stars, in twilight's sigh,
Celestial veils drift softly by.
In the hush, the cosmos gleams,
We wander lost in kindred dreams.

The sky's expanse, a canvas wide,
With whispered secrets of night implied.
Each glowing orb, a story spun,
Of timeless love, and hearts as one.

Veils of starlight, weaved so fine,
In cosmic dance, your hand in mine.
Together we forge a path so clear,
Through celestial wonders, we persevere.

In every twinkle, a promise shines,
Of moments cherished, our hearts entwined.
As night unfolds its velvet grace,
In the twilight folds, we find our place.

And though the dawn will chase us hence,
In starlit dreams, we find our sense.
For in the night, our spirits soar,
In celestial veils, we seek for more.

Beneath the Gales of Time

Upon the winds, we drift and sway,
Beneath the gales, the night and day.
In whispers carried on the breeze,
Echoes of life, like rustling leaves.

The clock ticks on, yet moments spare,
Each breath we take, a fleeting care.
Through silent storms, and sunlit grace,
In time's embrace, we find our pace.

The stories old, entwined with new,
In every heartbeat, a chance to view.
The past resides in memories' hold,
While futures dance like threads of gold.

So let us sail on tides of fate,
With dreams as guides, we navigate.
In the gales of time, we learn to trust,
In moments shared, in love we must.

With every gust, our spirits rise,
A timeless journey 'neath endless skies.
Together we weather the storms of night,
Beneath the gales, we find our light.

Veils of the Enigmatic Sky

Whispers of twilight softly fall,
Veils of mystery drape over all.
Stars flicker like secrets in flight,
Painting the dark with shimmering light.

Clouds drift like dreams across the scene,
Hiding the truths that lie in between.
The moon, a guardian, watches so near,
Embracing the night with a gentle cheer.

Comets chase shadows in a dance,
Carving new paths in a fleeting glance.
Nature holds secrets, ancient and wise,
Veils of the enigmatic sky arise.

The breeze carries stories untold,
Of longing, of hope, of hearts turned bold.
While stars keep a vigil, steadfast and bright,
Illuminating dreams on this mystical night.

We gaze upward, our spirits set free,
In the vastness, we find unity.
For beneath these veils, together we sigh,
Bound by the wonders that paint the sky.

Dance of the Enshrouded Spirits

In the meadow where moonlight glows,
Spirits entwine in an ethereal show.
With whispers of winds, they waltz with grace,
Floating like shadows in a timeless space.

Invisible threads pull them in lines,
Chanting the secrets of ancient designs.
Around the trees, they twist and spin,
Calls of the night pull them deeper within.

Veils of night drape softly around,
Embracing the hush, a mystical sound.
They gather in circles, their laughter a song,
In the heart of the night, where they all belong.

The stars blink in rhythm, a celestial beat,
Nature's own orchestra, tender and sweet.
Each movement a story, a tale to be spun,
A dance of the spirits, forever begun.

With dawn creeping in, their revelry fades,
Yet echoes remain in the sun's gentle blades.
For even in silence, their essence is found,
In the whispers of leaves, they're forever bound.

Shadows of Starlit Embers

In the depth of night, embers glow bright,
Casting shadows that dance in the light.
Flickers of warmth in the dark, they gleam,
Whispers of stories that drift like a dream.

The air is thick with tales unsaid,
Memories lingering where sorrows have tread.
In the stillness, secrets weave through the air,
Entwined with the echoes of moments laid bare.

Stars watch from above, so distant, so vast,
Guardians of time, holding shadows of past.
With each crackle and pop, a new tale is born,
In the glowing embrace of the break of dawn.

Beneath the cloak where the embers ignite,
Dreamers gather, conjuring light.
As the shadows take flight, we are carried away,
Into the realms where the night meets the day.

With every flicker, the silence dissolves,
In the heart of the embers, our spirit evolves.
For shadows of starlit embers shall shine,
Igniting the soul, transcending all time.

Beneath the Serpent's Breath

In the jungle's heart, where whispers entwine,
A serpent slithers, ancient and divine.
Beneath the emerald shadows it weaves,
Secrets of wisdom in tangled leaves.

Echoes of thunder rumble and play,
The serpent's breath guides night into day.
With scales that shimmer like dew on the grass,
Glimmers of mysteries, deep as they pass.

The dance of the branches sings low and sweet,
As the creature of myth finds its path beneath.
Guarding the stories of those who roamed,
It weaves through the twilight like roots in the loam.

Under moonlight's gaze, its power abounds,
In the still of the forest, ancient sounds.
Wrapped in allure, it watches and waits,
With wisdom of ages, it softly relates.

For beneath the serpent's breath, we find peace,
A harmony swirling, a timeless release.
The jungle embraces each being with grace,
In the heart of its depths, we all find our place.

Luminous Trails in the Midnight Sky

Stars scatter like whispers, soft and bright,
They weave through the darkness, pure delight.
Galaxies spin in a cosmic embrace,
Guiding lost souls through the vastness of space.

A comet streaks by, painting the night,
Chasing dreams that dance, taking flight.
Each twinkle a promise, a soft, sweet sigh,
In the tapestry woven, our hopes will lie.

The moon watches over, a sentinel wise,
Casting silver shadows across the skies.
With every breath taken, the universe swells,
In the heart of the cosmos, every secret dwells.

Whispers of starlight beckon us near,
To wander through wonders, to conquer our fear.
In luminous trails, we find our way home,
In the midnight expanse, forever we roam.

So gaze at the heavens, let your spirit soar,
For in every glimmer, there's so much more.
Life's journey illuminates with each passing glow,
As luminous trails in the midnight sky flow.

Shadows Dancing with Fiery Hearts

In the stillness of night, shadows play,
Twisting and turning, in a mystical ballet.
Fiery hearts beating, a rhythm so grand,
Moving together, hand in hand.

Embers flicker with whispers untold,
Stories of passion in the dark unfold.
With every step, a spark ignites,
In the dance of the shadows, love takes flight.

Veils of darkness cloak the dreams we chase,
Entwined in the light, we find our place.
With fiery intensity, we light up the skies,
In the shadows that sway, our essence lies.

The night breathes life, with a gentle sigh,
Our spirits entwined, as the world goes by.
In the rhythm of hearts, a fierce symphony,
Shadows embrace, a passionate decree.

So let the shadows dance, let the embers glow,
In the warmth of the night, let our love overflow.
With fiery hearts dancing, in every part,
The shadows will hold the light of our heart.

The Twilight of Mystic Flame

As twilight descends with a gentle grace,
Mystic flames flicker, illuminating space.
A palette of colors, soft and serene,
In the embrace of dusk, all emotions convene.

In the coolness of evening, whispers arise,
Carried by breezes under darkening skies.
The world holds its breath, as day meets the night,
In the twilight's soft glow, everything feels right.

Reflections of warmth in the fading light,
Chasing away shadows, dispelling the fright.
With each lingering moment, the magic remains,
In the twilight of flame, all sorrow wanes.

The horizon ablaze with a mystical hue,
Drawing in dreamers, inviting the few.
To gather their stories, in twilight's embrace,
As the mystic flame dances, revealing its face.

So cherish the twilight, the spaces in between,
Where the day meets the night, and all that's unseen.
In the warmth of the flame, let your spirit reclaim,
The beauty of moments in twilight's sweet frame.

Hues of an Unfathomed Sky

Above the horizon, the colors ignite,
Hues of wonder in the still of the night.
Blues blend with gold, a painter's delight,
In the palette of dreams, take flight.

Clouds drift lazily, like whispers of air,
Each shade holds a secret, a tale to share.
With every brushstroke, the universe sighs,
In the canvas of darkness, where true beauty lies.

Streaks of crimson dance, vibrant and bold,
Telling of stories that beg to be told.
As stars waken slowly, their glittering gleam,
They punctuate moments, weaving our dream.

In hues of azure, the soul finds its peace,
As night draws its curtain, the chaos will cease.
Let the shades wash over, in silence, we stand,
In the unfathomed sky, we find common land.

So gaze at the heavens, lose track of time,
In the hues of twilight, life's essence does rhyme.
In the depths of the night, let your heart take wing,
For in hues of the sky, the universe sings.

Enigmatic Flare Amidst the Twilight

In shadows deep, a spark ignites,
Mysteries dance in fading light.
Colors blend, the night unwinds,
Whispers soft, the heart will find.

Stars emerge, a velvet sea,
Secrets held in harmony.
Silent songs, the moonlight sings,
Dreams take flight on fragile wings.

Time stands still, the world apart,
A moment's grace, the beating heart.
In twilight's glow, the truths laid bare,
Enigmatic flare fills the air.

Ghosts of the Tempest's Heart

Thunder roars, the sky doth cry,
Whispers haunt the winds that sigh.
Shadows creep where memories dwell,
Echoes rise from tempest's swell.

Lost in dreams of stormy nights,
Phantom figures dance in fright.
Waves crash on the shore's embrace,
Ghostly forms in nature's race.

Steam and fog, a chilling breath,
Life and death, a dance with death.
In the storm's heart, secrets flow,
Haunting rhythms, a ghostly show.

Silken Threads in a Chaotic Breeze

Frayed edges of a woven tale,
Softly drifting, lost and pale.
Chaos swirls in vibrant hues,
Silken threads weave tranquil views.

Colors clash, yet find their peace,
Harmony in each release.
Moments caught in gentle sway,
Breeze that carries dreams away.

Fragile weaves in nature's hand,
Guiding hearts through shifting sand.
Tangled paths, yet so divine,
Silken threads, our fates entwine.

Reveries of the Night in Fading Light

As daylight wanes, the dreams ignite,
Whispers linger, soft and bright.
Stars awaken in velvet lace,
Guiding souls to a sacred space.

Echoes linger, the night unfolds,
Stories ancient, gently told.
In twilight's grip, we find our way,
Reveries of night lead to day.

Memories bathed in silver gleam,
Life is but a fleeting dream.
In fading light, our hearts take flight,
Embracing all the magic of night.

www.ingramcontent.com/pod-product-compliance
Ingram Content Group UK Ltd.
Pitfield, Milton Keynes, MK11 3LW, UK
UKHW021435160125
4146UKWH00006B/103